Spectacle

PANHANDLER
BOOKS

UNIVERSITY OF WEST FLORIDA | PANHANDLERMAGAZINE.COM

# SPECTACLE

✦ LAUREN GOODWIN SLAUGHTER ✦

Panhandler Books | Pensacola, Florida

27  26  25  24  23  22   6  5  4  3  2  1

Library of Congress Control Number: 2021949694
ISBN 978-0-9916404-6-1

Panhandler Books
University of West Florida
11000 University Parkway
Pensacola, FL 32514
http://www.panhandlermagazine.com

University of
West Florida

For my sister

# Contents

# Acknowledgments

Deep and heartfelt gratitude to the National Endowment for the Arts for the support that allowed me to complete this collection. Thank you to so many friends and mentors for guidance and encouragement, especially, Tina Mozelle Braziel, Daniel Torday, Wendy Reed, Kerry Madden, and Charlotte Pence. Thank you to my wonderful colleagues at the University of Alabama at Birmingham. Infinite thanks to Jonathan Fink at Panhandler Books for publishing this collection and for always being an absolute joy to work with. Thanks to my husband, Ben, and children, Sam and Eleanor. Love and thanks to my sister, Kate, for encouraging me to write about trichotillomania. Thanks to my parents for their love and support, always. Overwhelming thanks to Rineke Dijkstra, whose photographic portraits inspired and helped shape this book, and who graciously allowed me to include those portraits here.

Finally, thank you to the editors of the following publications in which some of the poems (some in slightly different forms or under different titles) in this book appeared previously:

*32 Poems*: "Kolobrzeg, Poland, July 26, 1992"

*Carolina Quarterly*: "Cookery" and "Kitchen, 5 a.m."

*Canary*: "Ghost Forests"

*Construction*: "Sometimes You Just Have to Grow Up"

*The Doll Collection* (Terrapin Press): "I Hit My Sister with the Speak-N-Spell"

*Eleven Eleven*: "On Seeing the Girl at the Gym with Bald Patches" and "Trich: What My Sister's Treatment May Involve"

*Hampden-Sydney Poetry Review*: "Ode to the Funeral Program for My Friend Mark's Mom"

*Hayden's Ferry*: "Asteroid Heading to Earth: Will Your Cell Phones Go Out?"

*Kenyon Review Online*: "Syringe Training, Home Visit"

*Love's Executive Order*: "The Days and Weeks Ahead"

*Nashville Review*: "Elegy for Michael Friedman" and "*Julie, Den Haag, February 29, 1994*"

*ONE*: "The Fourth Bomb Threat; Birmingham JCC"

*On the Seawall*: "Mom Turns 79 during the Global Pandemic"; "The Neutral Ones" and "Shut Up Amy Cooper"

*Pandhandler Magazine*: "Boner"; "The Chemistry of Color"; "Birthday Parties"

*Phi Kappa Phi Forum*: "In Praise of Dark Matter"

*Pleiades*: "Pulse"

*PoemMemoirStory*: "With My Sister in the Bathroom"; "Before *The Birth of Venus*"; "Euphemisms"; "Waiting for Another Call from My Sister in the Middle of the Night"

*RHINO*: "Alice the Corpse Flower Blooms at the Chicago Botanic Garden" (Winner of the 2019 Founders' Prize)

*Sporklet*: "Ode to the Frog in Her Throat"

*SWWIM*: "*Vila Franca de Xira, Portugal, May 8, 1994*"

*Sugar House Review*: "In-Flight: Philadelphia to Birmingham" and "*Self Portrait, Marnixbad, Amsterdam, June 19, 1991*"

*Valparaiso Poetry Review*: "Tornado Season"

# SPECTACLE

"I was always trying to find the uninhibited moment."

~DUTCH ARTIST AND PHOTOGRAPHER, RINEKE DIJKSTRA


"Cries galore

come from the water-closet door,

from the dropping-plastered henhouse floor,


where in the blue blur

their rustling wives admire

the roosters brace back their cruel feet and glare


with stupid eyes

while from their beaks there rise

the uncontrolled, traditional cries."

~FROM "ROOSTERS," BY ELIZABETH BISHOP

**I**

# Alice the Corpse Flower Blooms
# at the Chicago Botanic Garden

In September, 2015, thousands gathered to see Alice the Amporophallus, one of the Chicago Botanic Garden's "corpse flowers," named for their rancid stench, when she unexpectedly bloomed.

And what woman

hasn't been thus
gathered round,

a mob of cell phones
raised like torches

poised to snag the spectacle

that is her efflorescence—
pompons peeping out

(glimpse of thigh
or thong)

ovules swollen
with her fertile redolence?

Because smell is indifferent
to video or maybe more

the dare you take
to taste the sour milk

a queue of tourists forms
to step right up to Alice's enormous

sex and nozzle in—
whole heads will disappear

in a cunnilingual pantomime
the wincing faces say

reeks of rotting flesh,
or fish, or death.

~

We use real words
at our house, not prim

approximations, not
the *birdie* of my childhood,

or *girly bits*, or *vee-vee*,
or *hoo-hoo*, or *kitten*,

yet despite my professorial directives
my young daughter

refers only to her *private*—
that is private

in the singular, like signage
on her bedroom door

years from now, and as if
understanding, somehow,

she must enlist
a part of herself always

to serve as her own soldier,
her very own private,

her protector,
and I won't correct her.

II

## Julie, Den Haag, February 29, 1994

~After the photograph by Rineke Dijkstra, from her New Mothers series

The shock of sudden motherhood
flares Julie's face like fireworks

willowing. A single hour
post-delivery, her infant's skin

still burns with birth, the crimson
offset by mother's pale exhaustion.

Their dual nudity caffeinates the frame.
How did she cull the strength to stand

before the camera? Must be her first time
holding baby—any baby?—the way

she smashes the thing to her body
like ill-positioned groceries—

jumble of soup cans, milk, and melons
she will not drop no matter what.

I wonder if that little mouth can breathe.
But this is what a mother does, a mother

holds. Even caught in labor's daze
I knew to call my squirming howl

*Beautiful, so beautiful . . .*

before oceans of hands swept my boy
onto a metal tray to measure things.

My husband watched his eyelashes
unfurl. Then, gratitude,

a new kind of female gratitude,
for the nurse who knew to find me

two cups of strawberry ice cream
I consumed with a miniature paddle,

loving each slide of sweetness,
my legs earthquaking under the blankets.

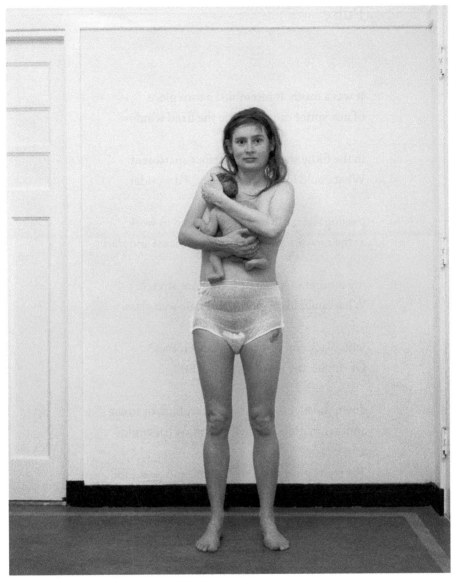

Rineke Dijkstra, *Julie, Den Haag, February 29, 1994* [original photograph is in color].

# Pulse

It was a moth. It resembled a torn piece
of newsprint caught inside the fixed window

in the filthy stairwell of our first apartment.
What could live in such a place, I'd wonder,

passing the moth on my way down to work
at the new teaching gig, outfit in *blouse* and *slacks*—

my mother's words—that did not stretch.
What could live in a world of hair-web glass,

with black and blackening stuck leaves?
Of course, the moth was dead. Still,

down the flights for prenatal aerobics, or to see
another matinee alone I'd think, What could?

The stairs grew thick with grime and dust.
A ball of something seemed to grow itself.

I starved no matter what and woke each night
to smear globs of Peter Pan on anything

we had. There was no air for me that August.
Yet, this pear to avocado to gourd-big boy became.

I pressed against the pane. This moth has legs,
I finally saw, skinny, with joints, and furred,

like those pussy willows I once named
and rubbed against my cheek at grandma's house.

And the creature's wings were more than paper, after all—
spun and flying-full and, somehow, real.

There that thing sat, for years. The baby charged
into a boy. Then, his worrying began.

Plonking past it on our way to school—
his jumbo pack tush-thwacking—or to the store

for milk, my son fret to the isolate of tears
pleading for me to free the moth. It's scared, Mama,

Mama, do something. Oh, that little guy's fine,
I tried, Love, see, he's only sleeping—do you know

the word, nocturnal? He did, and didn't buy it.
He wants out, my son persist. Still, I could not

form those words. His dog, his bed, his sister—
my moth misses the clouds, he drummed.

I kept, *it's dead,* until dead seemed the best,
most agreeable option. Is this failing

somehow, my success? Willow tree
sways of quiet next. Seesaw simple

breath. We came and went and, for months,
hardly looked at all. Shape meant shape

meant shape. Even the radio seemed safe.
The darkest clearing

yields the brightest stars. My son knew this
of the universe. This is what I taught him.

Then came the first-grade field trip
to Samford Planetarium. Circles black

with circles, tiers of disbelieving kids.
The sun—the sun will die, Mom?—

as he sprint off the bus, up the stairs
and to me, spilling Luna the Lion,

snack-fish confetti and all those cheerful
illustrations of smiling stock houses

puffing smiling white smoke. Oh, Sweetheart,
not die (did I try to chuckle?). Again, not die,

exactly. You see, the sun is not really alive
in the way we understand. More, the sun

will cease to burn. More, this gorgeous
heat this love just morphs to ice and fails

and falls, its glimmering tail sweeping
the impossible, brief shock of us—

our morning cuddle, your sleep-stale hair
beside me. Don't fear, it is more like that.

It's like that window painted shut that was never ours
to open. This isn't even our apartment.

Suddenly: nothing
or—a sound—one name—goes loose

in the place—then, music names on air
from the kitchen:

*Amanda Alvear; Oscar A. Arancena-Montero*

in that verified sober newscaster voice,
too careful to annunciate

*Rodolfo Ayala-Ayala*

the throb of knowing, always,
what comes next—

*Antonio Davon Brown*
*Angel Candelario-Padro—*

# Kitchen, 5 a.m.

1.

Through the blue kettle's first sigh of steam
my daughter is my mother swept            beyond the white breakers.

2.

Before a thing cries I will catch it.

3.

*Down? Want milk? Want up?*
I Charleston for a laugh in the fridge's spotlight.

4.

I strains through the peepholes of colanders.

5.

Bleachers of eggs go blank at this mother burlesque.

6.

In the absence of applause: forever percolates.

# Cookery

**1.**

It's terribly confusing, how the bottle of milk
was, was, still was, then went. Where did it go?

Her doll face contorts with disappointment
in me (You allowed this to happen).

*More?* I cartoon, guzzling
my sour garlic thumb. *Do you want more?*

For these hacked carrot torsos
and unwhorled onions, soup

is the only ambition. Futile food.
I'll just boil it to oblivion.


**2.**

The revolving rush of children
always going for the slide always

was too much for me; concealed
by the oak's arithmetic-ed hearts,

I'd watch every last kid launch.

In class, the answer was an ember smoking
gibberish. Smoke, my eyelet dress. Silence,

symmetrical. *Such a nice, sweet girl*
stuttered the yearbook scrawls.

Daughter, say more.

# Birthday Parties

Balloons set free over broccoli trees
equals tragedy for this birthday boy

with a name I squint for but can't quite pull
from his screaming

and these fluttery decorations
bound to every bare limb. One thing:

he's not mine. Mine stoically stirs orange fish
into her ice cream

at the picnic table wrecked by spilled cups
and SpongeBob cake crumbs

the paper cloth shred by claws it seems—oh look
how that dirty plate lifts with a wind gust

and sails through the bee-filled air
to land on that mommy's face! Her name

also escapes. Who has had their Lexapro today?
Not I. Not that mommy.

If I could escape from behind these sunglasses
I might go to this woman in workout gear

not so unlike mine and ask if she, too, is a poet
in disguise. We'd compare our kids' vaccinations

and strategize for when our wee ones—
milked and tucked in tight—gasp that this all

ends. Lullaby of choice? *Bye-Bye Baby*?
Too morose but, *Hush Little Baby* is broken things.

When music fails does she, too, deflect
the way good parents do and ask her kid to count

each green and glowing star above the bottom bunk
as if they won't unstick? The glob

of icing in her hair—what might
this woman write if I reach

with these similarly flawed instruments
and try to untangle it?

# The Fourth Bomb Threat; Birmingham JCC

In early 2017 over one-hundred Jewish Community
Centers in the U.S. received bomb threats.


This morning, with my daughter, on the drive
I felt that familiar twinge
again, and when


I left her in the brightness
of her classroom


with its miniature library
and many-potted kitchen and brimming bin


of farm animal costumes
plus a bear


and watched her go


to embrace her very best friends,
the twins, Jozie and Elon—


their hands pressing so softly
where the other's wings should be—


that twinge turned to fire
choked
by logic.


I am the stupidest of all the stupid mothers.
Everybody knows that

even, if, in an engine voice

a robot phones your child's school
and assures you, yes,

a bomb
has been planted
that will slaughter every last sleeping baby,

if that raging automaton

was really going to pull his switch
he wouldn't give the plan away

first.
Use your brain, woman. Use your noggin.

"Have the best day, darling!"
I'm trying

to discern the Exit light.

I find the long, dim,
ever-lengthening
corridor

between us.

Dragging, with lead shoes,

I peruse the walls
plastered with kid artifacts:

stapled cut-out heads of children

stuck on melting snow bodies;
    a garbled chain

    of torso-less hands of many-races;
                    indecipherable family

    portraits:

          pods of warped circles
          with flat smiles

     and scratched, mistake hair
     pierced
        by appendage rods.

    I continue, I must,

to my car,
              but cannot, I cannot

stop my heart, my prayer:

When it comes, God,
       let me be       here.

# The Chemistry of Color

In this course, we discuss the underlying physical processes that are involved
in the production of light and the ways in which its interaction with matter
leads to the colors we see in the objects that make up the world around us.

~ HAVERFORD UNIVERSITY SYLLABUS


We all bleed the same red blood of patriots, we all enjoy the same glorious
freedoms, and we all salute the same great American Flag.

~ DONALD TRUMP


There's always one natural sciences major
in the back of my lit class between the note-taking athletes
with fold-up legs and the dude who doesn't read
but hurls opinions at the lectern where I don't impress
anyone. My pit-stained blouse and marble-mouth, my joke
that never really finds a punch line, the stutter I reveal
in my favorite Bishop poem dazzle the science major
least. Who cares for my well-rehearsed musings honed
in the shower before silent, shampoo soldiers?
Before cracked windshields and mugs yawning?
*Like keys, the remote. One lonely sock. Class, what else in your life*
*exits to be lost?* Queue my fed-up pre-med's eye-roll,
book spread baldly to work with a lab component.
I could dry erase something—my student's eyes—
if the evidence wasn't so clear: each morning a new child
face-down on the beach, a child we won't hear
screaming from a cage. Across campus some maze mouse—

*Mus musculus*—on its back grew a real human ear.
Might it one day replace the plugged, went ones?
Poor mouse, poor all of us. My student's syllabus
for The Chemistry of Color pledges that glare
upon a thing will alter one's view, proven with chameleon
analysis and make-your-own Lava Lamp experiments.
A color-flipped pic of the American flag will exhibit
the trick of afterimages by making you stare real hard
first at black, blue, and yellow with black stars.
Then find the country you knew by closing your eyes.

## Vila Franca de Xira, May 8, 1994

After the photograph by Rineke Dijkstra, from her series of portraits of los
forcados. In the final event of a Portuguese bullfight, young men known as los
forcados use their bodies to exhaust and subdue the bull in a kind of dance
called pega de caras.


It was me or the bull
as it always is. The bull

with his brute-breath
and steam, fear that smells

of a father's knowing
his smaller son can take him

and will. Offer to bow
to the beast. Offer the dreams

in your skull, the Praia
de Benagil sunlight flaring

through a hole. Time is a boy
I can almost reach—

a kite flown, the blue-tiled floor
of my faraway mother

stampeded with footprints.
I came here for the question

answered by the crowd's
ovation: a man now, must

I have blood on my face
to be seen.

Rineke Dijkstra, *Vila Franca de Xira, May 8, 1994* [original photograph is in color].

## Self Portrait, Marnixbad, Amsterdam, June 19, 1991

After the photograph by Rineke Dijkstra

"I came out of the swimming pool and looked in the mirror and I took
my goggles off, and it looked like I was crying. I thought, maybe I should
make a self-portrait."

~ THE ARTIST, IN AN INTERVIEW WITH BLOUIN ARTINFO

After a brutal bike spill
    she was ordered to swim

herself well, and behold
    the breadth of that exhaustion:

fried goggle-sunk eyes,
    ruddled cheeks, spent limbs

that hang like a marionette's
    from her close-to-transparent

bathing suit. Replicating white
    wall and floor shower tiles

seem to try to box her inside
    but she's oh-so-very out-

of-the-lines. She's wrecked.
    In the now double-whiteness

of the Guggenheim, seized
    by the same exoskeletal twitch,

I feel a fissuring of the frame
      of experience. This gallery

is the tissue-skinned matron
      —her red helmet hair—

gripping the fist of her grandson.
      It's the whispering knot

of teens forced into
      one more dumb field trip

and the infant sucking her mother's
      bead necklace as the woman's

instinctual hips urge her child
      to sleepiness. Beyond, labyrinthine

hallways lead to the Impressionist rooms'
      careful arrangements

of peaches and pitchers, so cool
      in their pretty precision.

What bounty, order, and polish
      there is in this world

to resist. What pulsing temptation
      to twist oneself past

indelicate grace toward
      the safeness of a still life.

Rineke Dijkstra, *Self Portrait, Marnixbad, Amsterdam, June 19, 1991* [original photograph is in color].

III

# In Praise of Dark Matter

"Dark matter is a hypothetical invisible mass thought to be responsible for adding gravity to galaxies and other bodies.[ . . . ] This mass doesn't appear to affect normal matter significantly in any other way—such as by absorbing or emitting photons—making it completely 'dark.'"

~ SCIENCE ALERT


At first it seems unreal: a substance
    we can't see that holds everything together,

ghostly clouds of whatever, a kind of
    theoretical glue hitching suns to their spots

with its gravitational effect that to us
    appears to interact with nothing. Light shoots

off a vase of daisies placed upon the table
    straight through this unknown force—

this something—smack into the simple
    human eye. How clumsy to assume air

alone suffused that space spanning
    the body and its desired dwelling.

But really, didn't I know it all along
    with the corners of my wide-open mouth

with the melon I keep pulling toward my lips
    the unfathomable energy waiting

for the exquisite biting-in
    must be more than emptiness, in fact is all

the tension in our brief, blood-filled
    experience? I am Lauren Slaughter,

blue-veined corpus of the heart, spinning
    on our shared planetary orbit. I feel you

and believe in this elegant dark theory,
    the starry hunger blooming between us.

# Elegy for Michael Friedman

> "Michael Friedman, an Obie-winning composer-lyricist who held
> numerous leadership positions around New York theatre companies,
> has died at the age of 41 . . . Friedman's death on September 9 followed
> complications with HIV/AIDS."
>
> ~ PLAYBILL

A nuthatch eats a grasshopper
on my driveway and I realize

this is a thing I've never seen
before. It's the kind of thing

you don't realize you've never seen
until you see it: the bug is on its back

and the bird's twig-thin foot clamps
the belly down as it pecks away

in cool, quick, jabs. For a moment,
I hope—just a leaf? But dawnlight shows

a dying green leg slowly pedal
through tiny air. A translucent,

ripped-off wing—
iridescent, shimmering—

lands beside the wheel
of my son's scooter

and I think of you, Michael,
who I barely knew but did,

some, in school, when we were young.
Senior year you put Auden's

*Musée Des Beaux Arts* to music
which we tried to sing in choir,

our teenage jaws unlocked around
*about* and *wrong* in the first line.

Your song's avant-garde sharps
put a tune to our brooding moods,

but what did I really know of suffering?
Like, I backed my nine-seater station wagon

with the sweet wood paneling
into your sister's car and cried

(your parents were so kind).

Plus, I was too tall, and David Cope
broke my heart, and all the other

getting-taller boys with wrists
I could circle with my fingers.

(You suffered: I will not guess.)

Space and depth; how does one
measure the distance between

where a person is and ends?
Take my son, for instance, how

the baby at my breast
just turned eight and likes eggs fried,

makes a solid corner kick, gels his hair
to "make it Elvis" I tell you

he will spend an hour under
the bathroom's harsh fluorescence

just to sculpt that perfect swoosh.
You settled into such a beautiful man,

the Google Image search reveals.
It's been over twenty years—

I mean isn't there always somewhere
to have to get to—and so I scour

all the voices—*Love and mercy*—
mourning you in finite characters online—

*Only Michael would know how to make sense of this*—

any limits on language seeming just as well, as
*No words* repeats

on your sister's timeline.
*No words, there are no words,*

for what we finally can see
we've never seen before

until we witness the tragedy
in lights because light has to

shine on this disaster: someone amazing
disappearing into the *music we'll never hear.*

* In italics: Twitter posts and Facebook comments

# Syringe Training, Home Visit

In the quiet voice I enforce all nights
          by this hour
my husband asks the nurse in
                              and would she like
some water
and shows her to the table where we've laid it
all out: the tiny vial,
the needles, the orange, a square of gauze
like timid dodge-ball hopefuls.
          Was that a crying noise?
We three share a look and sit.
                              One jewel
of sweat unlocks,
                    smears a strip down my too-rouged cheek.
          *No time, no time at all, you'll have this down*
she jabs the rind, greenish
                    my flesh
too is ill.
                              But once I culled a soul
          and my middle brewed it—a swimmer
boy with fly wing
                    skin like mine.
My turn next
with the syringe and there it is
          *Don't hurt, you'll see . . .*
                    the crying sound        again, I flash
down the hall to that sweet-smell dark belonging
to someone else.

# Tornado Season

Birmingham, Alabama

Before the raven raging
the sky—

backlit green—
seemed to leak

from the muted
April leaves.

Looking back,

how ill fit to see
a Trevi Fountain

blooming

in the darkening
brume, close

the window and return
to our adobe-spiced kitchen,

a stack of Whitman
essays, my blue mug steaming

with the last ginger tea
and remember

to put *my tea*
on the store list.

# Boner

~ For Ed

Once upon a time it was the summer
of Serena's pool—

amoeba-shaped and deep
behind her house with no parents

for miles, a place
we could chain-smoke

and drink beer until our mouths
felt metallic

as we cannonballed
into the too-chlorinated fog.

Ed arrived after football practice
sweaty and salt-smelling

with soaked blonde curls
because he wasn't dead

at sixteen
the way he'd be at twenty-eight.

So, it was also the summer of Ed alive
or that's what it has become

distanced from that August
of his slight lisp

when he said, *Lauren.*
His tongue got caught

upon another word: *years*
or maybe, *please.*

Knotted beneath
the diving board

I found beneath his bathing trunks
the thing I'd heard about

—a boner—seemingly simple
shape of want. Ed is and has been

bones by now, nothing
to taste and not at rest

with a cat or child,
books spread around

the favorite chair recalling
a kind of love or, more, everything

that fills a life with blood.

# Ghost Forests

"As sea levels rise so do ghost forests."

~ THE NEW YORK TIMES

Like bare hands
reaching

from below
the grave, these

once-magnificent
woods. Roots

that pulled
from this earth

are choked now
with salt water,

waters meant
for a life

of fish not
sunken seeds

and drowned
burrows. Cold

may no longer
come to this place

and yet the spine
shivers

to see branches
that could have

blessed shade
upon your

very own children
seem to keep reaching

for some
right word

in some right
language

human ears
can hear. Listen.

This is the silence
of loss. Air

does not whisper
through leaves.

Air that touches
nothing

has nothing
to say.

# Ode to the Funeral Program
## for My Friend Mark's Mom

As we sat there waiting for the service to begin
I pondered the sketch on your front cover

which in pencil showed the chapel we sat inside.
I wondered if looking hard enough through

the roughly-drawn windows I just might see myself
staring at your cover staring at your cover

and in this way go on forever. In heels I walk like a monster
but one must do what is required. Pearl earrings,

black dress, a clutch of tissues at the ready. Your heady
floral aroma I assumed a symptom of proximity

to incense. Your card stock was clearly superior
to some soggy Lost Dog flyer stapled to a poll downtown

but not a politician's sleek brochure
wedged between windshield wiper and the glass.

I approved of your soft, taupe hue so keenly
in emotional concert with the just-so lily arrangements

and subdued organ tunes coaxing friends and family
from the cloudless day inside to their long, wooden pews.

I might even conclude that you felt like an invitation
to carefully stick to the fridge with a favorite sports team magnet

saving the date for an event there's no choice but to attend.
Oh, your script in black, Book Antiqua font!

Each margin so perfectly standard! I wondered if Mark offered
his input on your design or just ordered some package deal.

I hoped he was happy or at least 100% neutral on it.
One thing I was glad about: a joyful pastel photograph

of the departed is often depicted—wind smearing their hair
or shimmering the leaves of background trees

which only underscores that joy and wind for this loved-one
never comes again. I was grateful for your lack

of such a photograph plus the helpful directions in its place.
Like, when the time would eventually come for us all

to stand or sit in the service you would deliver
that charge in clear, bold type. Your Lord's Prayer version

switched out "our debts" for "our sins" and I deem this worthy
of a detailed footnote but maybe no funeral program is perfect.

Consider the gloomy context: unlimited sealed darkness.
It was going to be super uncomfortable when

we began to rise, me in my new DSW patent leather heels,
but this was not about me. I had never met Mark's mom—

not that I remembered—and was here to support my friend
from college sitting in the front row beside his pretty wife

with their iPad-clutching toddler, Paw Patrol cartoon on mute.
Good for them, I thought. Good for all of us who find

even small ways to cheat which is when I began to wonder
when drinks might be served in this lousy saloon. Bourbon,

I craved though it turns me mean and at any moment now
wouldn't it be grand for the waitstaff to parade on in

donning cute tuxedo outfits to present me with the glory
of a shining silver tray stacked with hors d'oeuvres I'd not considered—

veggies julienned out of recognition, blobs of mystery
roe, weird aioli schmears, and while we're entertaining

go on and give me all the meat you've got. I want it gory, pulsing,
raw—blood from my lips, blood down my pale veined throat

and nothing can stop it—more and more—shoes streamed through
the chapel's front doors until every last pew was full. *Immortal Invisible God.*

*Holy Holy Holy!.* One rumpled, red-eyed lady forced to stand against
a wall considered you so carefully—her lacquered thumb

pressed deep into your middle, she shamelessly waved you back
and forth until your body made a fan to pant

upon her cheeks where tears took the blush off in stripes.
Kind of beautiful the way you changed for her

parched and raisiny fingers, those terrible, mauve-glossed nails
as she kept on trying for air, just a little more.

# Mom Turns 79 during the Global Pandemic

From the harbor
of their porch—twin figureheads
    beaming—
    Dad in his Hawaiian shirt
    Mom fresh from online yoga
with the virus
maybe

                     swirling through all of this
   empty space
   between us.
        We brought cake
I wore plastic gloves to frost
and a rainbow
     of sidewalk chalk
to scribble birthday tidings
on cement. The cards
        I made the kids make go into
        a CVS bag
   weighted with
   one small stone
and tossed from six feet
back to land
    before them.
   From the other side
        they wait
        to see who picks it up.
I take a picture
     to send my sister
of Mom blowing

the candles out, each flame
taken by our mother's life-giving breath.
My wish
is to reach for my parents—
to touch and to stay, all of us
vines-curled.
But even with the gift of ten more years—
twenty more—
one day the earth will have me
pressed
onto itself
body flat, splayed into a star shape
ear to the dirt and worms
from six feet above
listening across the distance.

# Shut Up Amy Cooper

"I will tell them that an African-American man is threatening my life."

~ AMY COOPER ON THE PHONE WITH POLICE DURING THE ENCOUNTER
WITH CENTRAL PARK BIRDWATCHER, CHRIS COOPER. CHRIS COOPER
ASKED THAT SHE LEASH HER DOG IN THE "BRAMBLE," A POPULAR
BIRDWATCHING SPOT AND AN AREA OF THE PARK WHERE LEASHING
DOGS IS REQUIRED.


"I'm not interested in being in a room full of white people talking about race—I
think they still need that conversation but I don't need to be in it."

~ EDUCATOR AND BIRDER TYKEE JAMES, ON THE NATIONAL AUDUBON
SOCIETY'S JUNE 2020 ZOOM DISCUSSION, "BIRDING WHILE BLACK: A
CANDID CONVERSATION"


I used *African-American*
because I'm a good person.

I used *African-American*
like any good, white, woman
calling 911 on a reasonable request.
I follow the laws like everyone else,

knowing I can afford to break them and live

in my Upper West Side apartment
stocked with eco-products because
I'm a good person who cares about glaciers
as long as I don't have to see them.

I could have had any dog I wanted.
I could have had a purebred thing.

Look how I've been made
to pull the collar so he can't breathe.

Tell me the essential differences
between a Swamp Sparrow and a Song
and I'll tell you how much I over-tip
at "ethnic restaurants."

Tell me which species of woodpecker
is the smallest in North America
and I'll cover my mouth with a mask
and claim it's for your protection.

Tell me how unsafe you've been made to feel
scanning the tulips for Tanagers
and I'll present this receipt
for causes that come with a hashtag.

You tell me to back away. But how
could I hurt you, a person I've hidden from
myself, who seems to believe

there's still beauty to find
amid these vines and switches?

# Lockdown, 2020

We bought my son a videogame console
so he could hang out with his friends and kill people.
Every morning I make the coffee stronger.
The sun looms ever closer. We lope, room to room,
scanning the floor for windowlight scraps—
warmth to touch—despite proximity directives.
I recall more hopeful days. How we kept on
driving to school the "kitty way" which was just an alley
with a "Cat Crossing" sign and that one cat that one time.
What I wouldn't give for some unfamiliar softness
but we've vowed not to touch anything. Gunfire
from the screen and small, furious voices—*Die!*
*You suck! Come on!*—ricochet off every shut pane
into my son's head. All our heads. The slack-jawed
backpack sits empty on the couch, graded tests
crumpled at the bottom. On replay out there, know-nothing
hummingbirds dive-bomb the empty feeder. How lucky we were.

# The Days and Weeks Ahead

"In the days and weeks ahead, we expect to see the number of cases, the number of deaths and the number of affected countries climb even higher."

~ WORLD HEALTH ORGANIZATION, MARCH 11, 2020

I broke my arm.
It doesn't matter.

Every poet is writing this
poem today.

What else can fill these
watchful hours?

Every dog is walked,
all the lawns are preened—

dandelions switched
with pansies placed

into soil rich as
death. My son flew

right on by me—
that's how it happened—

playing basketball
for homeschooling P.E.

*Normal stuff still goes wrong
in pandemics,* my doc friend texts.

Down I went.
Yesterday, before all this—

or maybe a decade ago—
I sobbed to my husband

in the shower because
I'm too young

for high blood pressure
but numbers don't lie

plus there's this eruption
feeling all the time.

Something is missing
from our marriage

I also may have said
as he loofah-ed my back

with his beard. What
could I have possibly

possibly meant? My tiny,
non-displaced fracture

that hurts like hell
is invisible even by X-ray

just implied by how
the blood gathers.

If not for the pain
and disruption, how easy

to pretend it's not happening.
Nothing to see or do

but wait. And then,
for the healing to begin.

# IV

"Tear my bright hair and scratch my praised cheeks,

Crack my clear voice with sobs and break my heart . . ."

~ SHAKESPEARE, "TROILUS AND CRESSIDA"

Rineke Dijkstra, *Lina and Bruun, Amsterdam, Dec. 7, 2016* [original photograph is in color].

## Lina and Bruun, Amsterdam, Dec. 7, 2016

After Rineke Dijkstra's portrait of two sisters

Her good side shines, my chin looks soft
in light that isn't real, but made—

I want to rip this black dress off.
Her good side shines, my chin looks soft

so I can play the plainer one glossed
to be what all the ribboned straight girls say.

Her good side shines, my chin looks soft
in unreal light the artist makes.

It isn't fair to keep us here
posed on a rug by gas-lit fire

like frozen, taxidermied deer.
It isn't fair to keep us here.

I'd like a sip of water.
I may be small, but she's the crier.

It isn't fair to keep us here,
but in our eyes? Pure fire.

# With My Sister in the Bathroom

"Trichotillomania is a body-focused repetitive behavior classified as an impulse control disorder which involves pulling out one's hair. Occurring more frequently in females, it is estimated that 1%-2% of adults and adolescents suffer from trichotillomania. In general, trichotillomania is a chronic condition that will come and go throughout an individual's life."

~ MENTAL HEALTH AMERICA

Our products were aligned by rank.
Passion fruit and pinkish

they committed to exfoliate us,
peel, pop, scrub, and squelch.

I was careful to apply my Jean Naté tonic
with a cotton ball even though it burned.

And we all declared the revolting
black strands spaghetti-stuck

to the sides of the sink, or tumbleweeds
in the corner to be the dog's.

# Euphemisms

*Picking,* we called it,
as if my sister's

black tangle
was an orchard

to harvest
using Mom's

tweezers.
I never saw

her do it,
just the chicken skin

aftermath
to sheathe

beneath the butterfly

scarf. I helped knot
the back, admonished

but ate only Cheerios,
O by O.

Dad smoked
his fingers

to nubs.
The dog's tail:

gnawed and bloodied.

~

Blue-to-blue—

hops my daughter en route
to the bathroom—

blue-to-blue-to-blue

tile (grey are hot lava,
turn us *ghost-es*).

She wants to know—
when we become ghosts

is that sleeping?

# In-Flight: Philadelphia to Birmingham

On the occasion of my mother's 75th birthday party

We spend the morning blowing up balloons,
the plastic colors filled with my coffee breath,

shellacked by the kids' unapologetic spit.
Flabby failed attempts litter the just-swept floor.

I feel along the wall for the nails we keep in place
to hang the rotating cheer of our Happy Birthday sign,

its drooping smile and matte, fading shine.
Without it, we simply could not celebrate.

Your descent, Mother. I am in it. I'm the air,
dry and flu-filled, whirling in place, I am dirt

sour tea in your Styrofoam cup, the in-flight
magazine's sleep machine bartering choices

of water sounds. I hear the river's directionless
dark. I watch your shimmering gold

numbers float to the ceiling: seven trailed
by five. They will catch in the reeling fan,

the kids fret, between cartoon commercial breaks.
Thank you for this flour to sift, eggs to beat,

the request for our family banana cake
best made with the brownest, overripe flesh.

Doing my best to prepare for this,
the fruit has been ruining for a week.

Gluey pulp in a bowl. The flies gather.

# The Paramedics

Dad got dizzy again, Mom reports,
thought it was the blood sugar so drank
some OJ but when the world still whirled
like a drop-kicked gyroscope and the stiff
smiles on our school portraits kept lurching
across the wall until his legs went soft
and she was out—P.T. for her shoulder,
ringer off—and there Dad was on the floor,
hands and knees, stuck, he dialed 911
and once more the neighbors of forty-plus years
watched the ambulance block our narrow
Philly one-way lined with duplexes circa nineteen hundred,
watched the paramedics slow jog on up to the house
pallbearing a stretcher, push open the door
with its always-broken knob to find Dad there alone
because his dog is dead, Harry the retriever
with a Jheri Curl we joked, for whom Dad
lined the floors with Inquirers since he pissed
and shit wherever he could barely walk
but was loved so much there will never be another—
can't do it again, watch a dog die and die until one day
you wake up having seen enough suffering
and heave him into the back of the Oldsmobile,
panting, hot, and try to pet with one hand, speed
downtown to the vet with the other—
way over the limit so you don't lose the guts
the way you have before enough of this beige
wall-to-wall carpet that realtor said would increase value
this will not be it, this will not be capital *I.T.*

in my cold, small house. Who would feed the birds out back?
Who would make my wife laugh in spite of herself?
Maybe nobody's daughters ever call and just text
emoji strings: ♥♥☺♣♥
cause when we speak I get gruff if they prod
about my drinking, smoking, digging in the knife
with talk of the grandchildren, how I'm their only Pop-Pop
and for them must learn to take better care.
Eat my rice cakes. Lay off all the ice cream and beer,
sit and let the oxygen fill my lungs, keep me here.
Mom calls. Says now Dad's sitting up eating Jell-O,
flirting with the nurses, calling them hon
when he calls them over to *flip the news off—ballgame's on.*

# Sometimes You Just Have to Grow Up

My OB says when I ask
about another little one to tend

this want bloom heart
stuck in a jar perfuming

the room with its flesh
stink until the whole family's sick,

all four of us. (Bounty already:
one girl, one boy

as prescribed.) I learn petals
fall off. Off and off onto

the counter tacky with spilled Os
milk and finger jam. The mad cat

meme says, *Go embrace life
somewhere else* which I quote

here as it pleases me
to do so. Seasons of one's life.

Season of indulgence. I indulge
my therapist with my accomplishments,

help myself to a tissue for each
until the box gapes back

in sudden emptiness. And yet,
Dr. Viv says, you're not happy.

Let's explore this. My mother
likes to tell a story called

All the Punishment You Needed
of the Cinderella birthday

I attended as a girl,
how I licked every last child's

cupcake clean of its beautiful
pink icing until nothing

was left and hid in the closet,
ill, filled with the sunrise

pinks, sunset pinks,
pinks of the inside of things,

the body inside
the beating body breathing

breathing
because because

# Waiting for Another Call from My Sister in the Middle of the Night

Curtain moonlight muscles through the trance
I'm trying busting lambs and fences. Her words

last night were wordless, all crescendo issued
for some lonesome air defense. I tried to be a stewardess:

*Something I can help with*? Then just started counting
the stuck kicks of grandmother's watch as she bawled.

That lunatic dog is still going on and on about it.
Chardonnay and Raisin Bran was dinner. Hunger

bores a supernova, leaves its dense core.
Bring her here.

# Trich: What My Sister's Treatment May Involve

Comes
the crawly

innervate,
half

ectozoon
half

head-clouds
platooned

into
chitterlings

their languid
collection

eclipsing
your landscapes,

gulp Prozac
fistfuls,

harness
those

horsefingers
jammed

at the gate—
tendons

igniting
torrid excreta—

with Freaky
Freezy

gloves
that once

revealed
a mountain

scene. Nightly,
on an empty,

cloak the scalp
wormings,

the warmness
orgasm

cache
of each

follicle

opera
translated:

nearer.
Failing all

else, find
a mirror.

# On Seeing the Girl at the Gym with Bald Patches

mowed
in neat streaks

through
her cheery ponytail—

negative space
clenched

by a hot pink
scrunchie,

nylon shorts
hissing

with each
ovaloid advance

on the elliptical—
my sister's eyes go

*I'm not alone*

greened:
girl's got guts

to sweat it out

that half hour
we just lost fixing

Kate's headscarf
in the Ladies' stall,

hunched,
whispering

through pins
caught in our teeth

like traitors.

# I Hit My Sister with the Speak-N-Spell

*Dog-Dog-Dog*
the cyborg

stuttered, voice
of a father

cross her porcelain
back lashed

with my loosed
raging. She vowed

to dye her hair
blonde, change

her name to *Lauren*.
I let my best friend

slap her, let her eat
my entire Easter basket

so she'd get fat.
And she just had to

get my same
Madame Alexander baby

with spy eyes
that shut

when we plonked
our dumb daughters

on block beds
to sleep, bound in covers

like mummies
    didn't she?

# Sister Dance Off

Last night we drank like assholes
   and you won
the *Beat It* dance-off glorifying

your third farewell this week.
   I watched
the disco ball divide you

into pocket-sized orbs, tried
   to catch and tuck
them away. Didn't work. Love

that cowgirl shirt. Pearlescent buttons
   of stars traced
our zigzag home, tailed by the neighbor's

ding-ing cat. You're heading back
   out West for another
unfit boy. By the door, I see the silver

hoop you dropped. But this special
   hand-sewn pillow,
of perfect weight and softness,

because my neck gets gnarled
   with poems,
you left on purpose.

# V

"Once I feel myself observed by the lens, everything changes."

~ ROLAND BARTHES, *CAMERA LUCIDA: REFLECTIONS ON PHOTOGRAPHY*

Rineke Dijkstra, *Vondelpark, Amsterdam, June 19, 2005* [original photograph is in color].

# Vondelpark, Amsterdam, June 19, 2005

After the photograph by Rineke Dijkstra
"What I like so much is that because her dress is red [ ... ] all the attention
goes to her, and he is sort of admiring her.
Yeah, it is her picture."

~ DIJKSTRA, IN AN INTERVIEW WITH ARTS PRACTICAL

As if lifted from Monet,
this teenaged couple lazing

at the park, dapples jeweled
forever on their hair

and places flushed
with almost kissing

or the heat. He lingers
with the lake shadows

behind, almost in a move
of chivalry opening

a door of air
to us beholding

her red dress plus
converse chucks

and gaze that never
slips or turns away

from ours and how we wish
ourselves to see.

# "Asteroid Heading to Earth: Will Your Cell Phones Go Out?"

~ Quote from a "Developing Story" banner on CBS News, February 15, 2013

1.

They say it's half the size
of a football field,

weighs more
than the Eiffel Tower,

more than even a Carnival
cruise ship whizzing

through space eight
times faster than a bullet.

Hold onto your smart phones,
it could slide into Earth's orbit

of satellites, fucking
our frequencies for days:

an Atari cartoon
shows Verizon sputniks

get thwacked
by the imminent

shape. But it won't hit us,
we're assured, over clips

of *Armageddon:* Bruce Willis
geared up in astronaut stuff

diverts the ball blazing
straight for New York.


2.


It's more than hype
today in Chelyabinsk,

where the long-poisoned
river is barbed-wired

still and still children
get born without hands

sometimes—a shooting rock
like thirty Hiroshimas blew out

twenty football fields of glass.
*It's once-and-a-lifetime, a Cosmic Gold Rush!*

CNN's "Meteor Hunter"
skyped. *Well, can't escape fate,*

one farmer affirmed
into the camera's dilation.

# The Neutral Ones

My daughter's fed up with getting called boy.
She wants to trade in her brother's short hair

and hand-me-down athletic shorts
and polo shirt with the collar popped

for picture day. She wants to replace her handsome
smile for never explaining herself again.

*How many girlfriends you got?* I imagine the photographer
will tease as my daughter scans the room

for that teacher on a field trip who scolded her
for using the wrong restroom. She prefers

the neutral ones with half-skirted
stick figure signs

where everyone belongs and can be hers
as the sky is hers. Eleanor. My daughter

reveals she is about to cry when red stains streak
across her cheeks and I swear I could

slit that teacher's throat with the teeth
of a tiny black comb. With my teeth.

I have learned to murder anyone, mother
that I am—a fool at Target with a Starbucks

and hangover scanning The Girls Section
for a get-up my kid could stomach—

something ribbon-free and sans *Princess*—
bulletproof, perhaps, in a pretty shade

of math, refusing to conform, and always
speaking up. My own bowl-cut childhood

was roly-poly bugs and jacks, jeans
with the knees ripped out going for the ball

and still the fluorescent glare in here
is brutal boomeranging between mirrors

and the blank-faced mannequins—my face—
my mascara—my strong legs—my desires

that strange morning years ago I woke up
out of time into a middle space

between dreaming and perception
and for a flash was no one, just me

without a body, a Lauren-y existence
before corporality snapped me back

to shape and brain, this sale rack place
of dumb graphic t-shirts. *Roarsome!*

says the T-Rex. *Hang in there!*
jokes the cartoon sloth. *They/them/theirs*

demand my gorgeous students, fierce
in polyester, violet fades, and fedoras,

fluid as the ocean and complex as the night
out of range of any manufactured light.

# Ode to My Daughter's Burden

My daughter says *Thank you*
*for thanking me* when I praise her
for putting her brother's empty dish
into the sink. My daughter wears
red shoes from the Boy's section,
the Scout haircut she likes and a Target
t-shirt that reads, *Brave*. She teaches
math to a class of stuffed bears
lined up on our kitchen floor, gives them
kindness for homework. My daughter hopes
she might be permitted to offer
the man we see sleeping under the bridge
school mornings her glass jar full
of tooth fairy coins. My daughter requests
buttered noodles but agrees to her age
in spinach leaves if I insist. It was she
as her grandfather grew skeletal
to always be the one moving closer—
her soft arm around his sharp shoulders.
He's in heaven now, according to her
teacher who lines up the class with sealed
bubble-mouths and sends home arithmetic
problems that call for carrying the tens
each time. I watch my daughter retreat
to her room and try so hard to solve
every one. I wish her questions for me
to clear her closed door—a sign
she won't go it alone. Ear pressed
I'll wait, willing my girl from a girl's call
to carry it all. To carry everything.

# Ode to the Frog in Her Throat

"There's Ransom in a Voice—/ But Silence is Infinity."

~ EMILY DICKINSON, POEM 1251


To the swell

                    before

                              sound,

          the bubble-up

                    of what she meant

but damn

                              that syllable

          got stuck again,                                        O

                                        before *ing*

          so when she goes

to sing

                              a plank comes out

on which she's told          to walk

                    but hands bound

                              can only wobble

between deck

                                                            and the sea

          of her beautiful

                                        idea

          now a speck

                                                  disappearing

into the dusk's

                    silver          current

                                        where twin-slunk

                              with the sun

her true intention

                    will be kept,    pressed to pearl-

silence.                                        And, safe.

# Kolobrzeg, Poland, July 26, 1992

From Dijkstra's Beach Portraits series. The series features portraits of
adolescents, "on the brink of adulthood," posed in bathing suits on the beach.

Like a daughter of Botticelli's goddess,
with her same demure tilt and glazed,

resigned gaze. Yet, Dijkstra's teen
seems to accept our scrutiny's full dimensions,

sponge our spotlight eyes, imbibe
the shimmer of our seeing her foiled

by that bleak lime bathing suit—nylon
tugged into position, empty scallops

where breasts will come and pull across
the bready paunch, high-cut thigh exposing

seduction's imitation. Floaty hands
appear anesthetized with being told to

station down her sides. Even the ocean's
silvery crests assume the posture we expect.

Only one delightful detail betrays
the composition: the girl's messy socks

of sand clinging to her ankles, as if off-stage
she is forgiven the joy of stomping

mermaids and castles.

Rineke Dijkstra, *Kolobrzeg, Poland, July 26, 1992* [original photograph is in color].

# Before *The Birth of Venus*

Who doesn't know her
molten spill, the hot locks

Zephyrus blew into style
perpetual, the graceful fistful

of split ends that hide the beauty's
newly-wooled pudenda?

But figure all those floating years
before the shell ship wrecked

her lazing in the tonsured sunset
of a cup, drifting unseen

on green swirling maybe
letting her lids shut in

fractals, her fingers dip and groove
that wet salt feeling for the touch

of the curious cloud strokes—vital, raw, briny—
divulged entirely.

# About the Author

LAUREN GOODWIN SLAUGHTER is an NEA Fellow in Poetry, the recipient of a Rona Jaffe Foundation Writers' Award, and author of the poetry collection, *a lesson in smallness*. She is associate professor of English at The University of Alabama at Birmingham where she is also editor-in-chief of *NELLE*, a literary journal that publishes writing by women. Find her at www.laurenslaughter.com.

*Author's Note*: Many of the poems in *Spectacle* are informed by my sister Kate's brave openness regarding Trichotillomania. For information about and resources for support for Trichotillomania and other Body-focused repetitive behaviors visit the TLC Foundation at https://www.bfrb.org.

# About Rineke Dijkstra

RINEKE DIJKSTRA was born in Sittard, The Netherlands in 1959. Since the early 1990s, Rineke Dijkstra has produced a complex body of photographic and video work, offering a contemporary take on the genre of portraiture. Her large-scale color photographs of young, typically adolescent subjects recall 17th-century Dutch painting in their scale and visual acuity. The minimal contextual details present in her photographs and videos encourage us to focus on the exchange between photographer and subject and the relationship between viewer and viewed. Her work has appeared has appeared widely. For more information about the artist and her work, please visit the Marian Goodman Gallery at mariangoodman.com.

Though presented in *Spectacle* in black and white, the original portraits by Rineke Dijkstra are in color. The photographs have been reproduced in *Spectacle* in black and white with permission from the artist. The Rineke Dijkstra portraits included in *Spectacle* are:

Rineke Dijkstra, *Julie, Den Haag, February 29, 1994* (page 13)
Rineke Dijkstra, *Vila Franca de Xira, May 8, 1994* (page 29)
Rineke Dijkstra, *Self Portrait, Marnixbad, Amsterdam, June 19, 1991* (page 32)
Rineke Dijkstra, *Lina and Bruun, Amsterdam, Dec. 7, 2016* (page 60)
Rineke Dijkstra, *Vondelpark, Amsterdam, June 19, 2005* (page 80)
Rineke Dijkstra, *Kolobrzeg, Poland, July 26, 1992* (page 89)